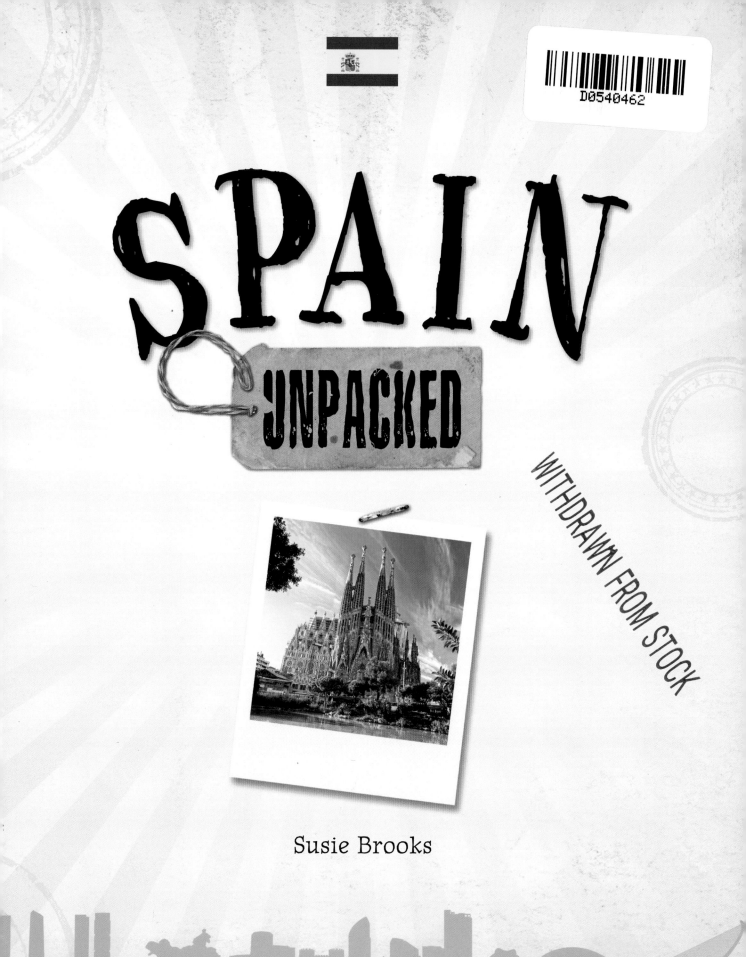

SPAIN

UNPACKED

Susie Brooks

First published in 2013 by Wayland
Copyright © Wayland 2013

Wayland
338 Euston Road
London NW1 3BH

Wayland Australia
Level 17/207 Kent Street
Sydney, NSW 2000

Editors: Annabel Stones and Elizabeth Brent
Designer: Peter Clayman
Cover design by Matthew Kelly

Dewey categorisation: 946'.083-dc23

ISBN 978 0 7502 7730 3

Printed in Malaysia

10 9 8 7 6 5 4 3 2 1

Picture acknowledgements: All images, including cover images and graphic
elements, courtesy of Shutterstock except: p5 © Getty Images; p9 © Getty
Images; p18 © Julio Donoso/Sygma/Corbis; p19 © Jack Hollingsworth; p24 ©
Wirelmage; p26 © AFP/Getty Images

The website addresses (URLs) included in this book were valid at the time of
going to press. However, it is possible that contents or addresses may have
changed following the publication of this book. No responsibility for any such
changes can be accepted by either the author or the Publisher.

Wayland is a division of Hachette Children's Books,
an Hachette UK company.
www.hachette.co.uk

Contents

Spain: Unpacked

Welcome to Spain, the European country that almost touches Africa! It's a colourful kaleidoscope of a place, thanks to a series of explorers and invaders bringing influences from around the world. Step this way for fiery flamenco, fun fiestas, tasty tapas and football fever - not to mention sunny beaches, snow-capped mountains and exciting cities. Some people call Spain the most exotic place in Europe - let's unpack and see if you agree!

Fact file

Flag:

Area: 505,370km²
Population: 47,370,600 (July 2013 est.)
Capital city: Madrid
Land Borders: 1,917.8km with three countries
Currency: The Euro

Spain

Useful Phrases

Hola/Adiós - Hello (informal)/Goodbye
¿Que tal? - How are you?
Muy bien, gracias - Very well, thanks
Por favor - Please
De nada - You're welcome
Me llamo - My name is
¿Habla inglés? - Do you speak English?
Hasta luego - See you later
¿Donde está el baño? - Where is the toilet?

Spanish (or Castilian) is also spoken in: Argentina, Bolivia, Chile, Colombia, Costa Rica, Cuba, Dominican Republic, Ecuador, Equatorial Guinea, El Salvador, Guatemala, Honduras, Mexico, Nicaragua, Panama, Paraguay, Peru, Puerto Rico, Uruguay, Venezuela... AND parts of Andorra, Belize, Gibraltar, Morocco, the Philippines and the USA!

CITY PASS

CITY PASS 2

CITY PASS 3

We know this Spanish artist as Picasso, but his full name was... Pablo Diego José Francisco de Paula Juan Nepomuceno María de los Remedios Cipriano de la Santísima Trinidad Martyr Patricio Clito Ruíz y Picasso!

128036 Rafaelnadal is an asteroid belt named after the Spanish tennis champion. Talk about out of this world!

A World of Their Own

Spain isn't a big country - but it can feel like a whole world in one! The people here live in 17 different regions. That means 17 different cultures, 17 regional governments, and four major languages too. Spain once ruled a great empire, and Greeks, Romans, Moors and other settlers all made their mark long ago. No wonder it's now such a varied place, with surprises wherever you go!

Moorish Moments

It's hard to miss the impact the Moors had on Spain. These North African Muslims swept through the country from the 700s, taking the arts, science and farming by storm. The Spain they ruled was rich and powerful – visit Granada's Alhambra for a glimpse of palace life back then. But Christians fought many ferocious battles with the Moors, and bit-by-bit their power came to an end.

 The Alhambra was built as a fortress and later converted into a palace.

The New World

It was two Catholic rulers, Ferdinand and Isabella, who drove out the last of the Moors. With their spare cash they paid explorers lik Christopher Columbus to take to the seas. Things looked good in 1492 when Columbus arrived in the Americas. They looked even better when his successors, the Conquistadors, conquered much of this New World and sent gold and other riches back to Spain!

Columbus wasn't actually Spanish – he came from Italy!

NO WAY!

Spain owns two cities on the northern coast of Morocco – Ceuta and Melilla. You can reach them both by ferry from mainland Spain.

Going it Alone

From 1936-39, a terrible Civil War shook Spain. The leader of the winning side was General Franco. He took power and ruled harshly, punishing people who opposed him and banning regional languages and culture. After his death in 1975, Spain became the monarchy it is today. Regions such as Cataluña and the Basque Country took up their own languages again. Many people in these parts would like to be separate from Spain.

People in Asturias party in their regional dress.

On the Ball

Ask a crowd of Spaniards what their favourite sport is, and the chances are most will say *fútbol*! Spain has some of the world's best football teams and a nation of keen supporters to match. For those who prefer wheels, or different balls, there are plenty of other strong contenders. From speedy cyclists to basketball and golf pros, Spain's sports stars are big and their fan bases even bigger!

NO WAY!

Real Madrid has won more European Cups than any other team and was named the best football club of the 20th century.

Real Madrid and FC Barcelona battle for the Spanish Super Cup.

He's an Ace

No one swings a tennis racket like Rafael Nadal. Known as 'Rafa' to his adoring fans, he plays with his left hand but writes with his right! This speedy Spaniard, once World Number One, has racked up 13 Grand Slam singles titles – including a record eight French Open wins. His success on clay courts has earned him the nickname 'King of Clay'. Well, he did start playing when he was three.

Nadal chose tennis, though he was a talented young footballer too!

Leagues Ahead

What's the world's richest football club? Real Madrid! And FC Barcelona is close behind. These two famous teams top La Liga, the world-leading Spanish league. The best players start early, and boys as young as six compete to train in the clubs' youth academies. No wonder Spain's national football team are European and World Champions!

Hands Up

When they're not kicking with their feet, the Spanish are pretty good at handball. In fact, they're World Champions in that too! Another popular sport is *pelota* – a traditional game from the Basque region. Here, players whack a ball against a wall using their bare hands or a curved, basket-like glove called a *chistera*. With bounces of up to 250km/h, it's been called 'the fastest sport in the world'!

Blink and you'll miss the pelota ball!

Highlands and Islands

Well yes, it does rain in Spain - but it's also one of the sunniest places in Europe! The south around Seville can get so hot it's been nicknamed 'the frying pan', while elsewhere in the country you can chill out on an icy mountain slope. High plateaus and sierras cover much of Spain, with rocky peaks descending to sandy shores. Visit for sun and sea or snow and skis - Spain really has it all!

You need high winds and strong arms to kitesurf!

Down at the Beach

You've probably heard of the Costa del Sol ('Costa' meaning 'coast' and 'Sol' meaning 'sunshine') but did you know Spain has nearly 5,000km of coastline? Many parts of it have descriptive names, such as Costa Brava (wild and rugged), Dorada (golden) and de la Luz (light). Spain has more than 500 blue flag beaches and people flock here to soak up the sun. In spots like southerly Tarifa, kitesurfers make the most of whipping winds too!

The Pyrenees join Spain and France and include the tiny state of Andorra.

Island Sun

Spain's islands have characters of their own. The Balearics are famous for their golden beaches, hills and caves – as well as non-stop parties and the invention of mayonnaise! On the volcanic Canary Islands you'll find black sand, formed from lava rock. They're closer to Africa than Spain, and are warm enough to attract beach-goers and grow bananas (about 400,000 tonnes of them) all year round!

Reaching a Peak

The Pyrenees, a range of mountains spanning some 430km, literally chop off Spain from the rest of Europe. The highest point is Pico de Aneto at 3,404m. Winters here are harsh, but if you wrap up warm you can enjoy the sparkling scenery and snow sports. In summer and autumn, try trekking, canyoning or take a bike. Competitors in the famous cycle race *Vuelta a España* need plenty of puff for the Pyrenees stage!

This sand isn't dirty – it's just made of volcanic rock!

NO WAY!

In ancient times the Canary Islands were known for their large dogs. Their name comes from *canes*, which means 'dogs' in Latin. Nothing to do with birds!

Sleepless Cities

They say that some cities never sleep - and there are plenty of those in Spain! Buzzing with businesses and late-night party people, the biggest are near the coast. About four in five Spaniards now live in urban areas, mostly in apartment blocks. There are expensive suburbs and shabby slums too. It's a mix of rich, poor, old and new - but you'll never be short of things to do.

NO WAY!

Madrid is Europe's highest capital city (667m above sea level) and the only one not built by a major river.

Magical Madrid

Slap bang in the middle of the country, Madrid is Spain's capital and its biggest city. More than 3 million people live here, and tourists can't get enough of the amazing museums, parks and bars. Hop on the Metro to visit Madrid's sights, from the city's hub, the Puerta del Sol, to the magical Royal Palace or the Casa de Campo – once a royal hunting ground and now a funpark and zoo.

You get a meal with a view in Madrid's impressive Plaza Mayor.

Sunny Seville

The Guadalquivir River cuts the city of Seville in two.

Take a high-speed train from Madrid and you'll reach Seville in two hours – but you might as well be in another country! While the capital sees scorching summers and freezing winters, this southern city is sunny for most of the year. Moorish architecture, flamenco music, bullfighting, tapas and marmalade oranges are all hallmarks here. Many people say it's Spain's most beautiful city – the proud Sevillanos certainly do!

Buzzing Barcelona

Want to see a cathedral that looks like a sandcastle? Come to Barcelona! Spain's second-largest city is famous for its quirky buildings designed by architect Antoni Gaudí. There's cutting-edge culture, and don't miss La Rambla – a lively market street packed with stalls, snacks and artists. It's one of the world's best beach cities too. About 7 million people take a dip off Barcelona's shores every year!

You can climb up inside Gaudí's Sagrada Familia!

Escape to the Country

There are parts of Spain where you're more likely to see a pig or goat than a person! Much of central Spain is sparsely populated, and you can travel for miles without reaching a town. Many people have abandoned their farms and villages to find city jobs, but others are finding ways to revive the countryside. For visitors who like peace and quiet, rural Spain is a dream come true!

You wouldn't want to sleepwalk in Arcos de la Frontera!

Life on the Edge

Building houses on hills can be a challenge, but in Spain they've mastered the art. Travel around Andalucía and you'll find villages clinging to some very steep slopes! Often set around a fortress, they've been there since Moorish times. Most are painted white, to reflect the sun's heat. For an even cooler home, just live inside the mountain – cave houses are popular round here too!

Iberian pigs like to eat acorns and are bred for their tasty ham.

Rural Retreats

Many people like to get away from it all in rural Spain. That's good news for the locals! Offering a bed and board to tourists is a useful earner, and if you can put them to work picking grapes or olives, even better. Agritourism is growing in Spain, with *casas rurales* opening their doors to guests from all over the world. Some foreigners have upped sticks altogether and moved to Spain to do this themselves!

Lots Growing On

It's a farming life for most rural Spaniards. Some just grow food for their families, while others go large with commercial crops. Citrus fruits, vegetables, nuts and olives cover much of the countryside. Pigs, goats and chickens roam the land. Grapes are another key product – Spain rivals Italy for the most wine exports, and has the biggest planted area of vineyards in the world!

To help pick grapes, visit Spain between August and October.

NO WAY!

Spain has at least 320 million olive trees – more than any other country! It produces about 40-60% of the world's olive oil, depending on the harvest.

Wild Spain

Animals thrive in Spain's gigantic wilderness areas. The country has more than 400 nature reserves, where creatures big and small can run wild. You could count more than 500 types of bird here, if you really tried, and at least 120 mammal species too!

There's no point chasing a Spanish ibex up a mountain — this horned, goat-like creature has nimble feet and short legs that can scamper up and down cliff faces at speed.

It's pretty rare to spot a wolf these days, but there are about 3,000 left in the Spanish wild. While you're waiting quietly, look out for wild boar and red and roe deer. They could be the wolf's next meal.

The Iberian lynx is critically endangered and now found only in areas of southern Spain. This is partly because this bearded wild cat only likes eating one thing – rabbit!

Chimney stacks, church spires, telegraph poles... these are just some of the places where white storks like to nest. The higher the better, as far as they're concerned!

About 600 years ago, camels from North Africa were brought to the Canary Islands. Now tourists can hitch a ride on them to see the isles.

Grizzly bears in Spain? Oh yes! But don't worry – the Cantabrian brown bear is one of the smallest types, and very shy. It's more interested in eating roots, fruits and insects than humans.

Spanish Life

You don't go to Spain expecting to be in bed at 8pm. Even midnight is early for some people! Spaniards eat late, sleep late and walk around the streets late. They love to chat and spend time with friends and family. The Spanish day is broken by a long lunch and snoozy siesta - shops close and things go a bit quiet. That doesn't mean we're talking lazy people - typical Spaniards like to be on the go!

NO WAY!

In Spain children get two surnames! The first comes from the father's side and the second from the mother's. What would yours be?

Folk dancing is part of the fun at this school in Seville!

Way to Learn

One thing that doesn't happen late in Spain is school! Lessons start at 9am, and there are earlier breakfast clubs for children whose parents need to get to work. Some schools break for two hours or more at lunch, when pupils can go home. The best thing is the long summer holiday – 10 or 11 weeks of freedom! Lots of kids go to summer camps, where there are activities from sports to art or cooking.

18

Family Fun

Whether they're playing in a park or strolling for an evening *paseo*, Spaniards love to hang out with their family – so much so that children get to stay up late too! Socialising is a big part of life, and if there's something to celebrate, nothing will get in the way. Luckily there are more bars and cafés per person here than anywhere else in Europe, where families can meet and spend time together.

There's no hurry when you're out for a family stroll!

Catholic Country

You'll probably agree, one birthday a year is not enough. Solution: celebrate your Saint's birthday too! About 70% of Spaniards are Roman Catholics, traditionally named after saints or other holy figures. Religion isn't as strict as it used to be here, but First Communion is still a big event for many children. Girls wear fancy dresses and boys put on smart suits. After the ceremony there's a big family meal.

Children take part in a Catholic Easter procession.

All You Can Eat

Fancy a doughnut dipped in hot chocolate for breakfast? If so, you're in the right place! Many Spaniards start the day with a quick sweet snack, making lunch their most important meal. Cooking is a popular pastime, and Mamá's favourite recipe is sure to pass down through the family. What goes in it depends on the region - touring Spain can be an adventure your tastebuds won't forget!

Home-grown

Food doesn't have to travel far in Spain. It's all about local ingredients, from tomatoes and fried fish in Andalucía to Catalonian sausages and Asturian white bean stews further north. You could spend a long time chewing on all the different Spanish hams and chorizos, and the variety of local cheeses is mind-boggling. One thing it's hard to turn your nose up at is olive oil – the Spaniards don't cook without it!

You'll be spoilt for choice in a Spanish ham shop, or *jamonería*!

Seafood paella is a popular dish in places around the coast.

NO WAY!

Imagine a paella big enough to feed 110,000 people! It has been done (in a VERY large pan) using 6 tonnes of rice, 12 tonnes of chicken and rabbit and 1,100 litres of olive oil!

Time for Tapas

When you don't eat dinner till late, tapas can tide you over! These mixed snacks are popular with drinks. Try:

Tortilla – a thick potato omelette (in Granada they sometimes throw in pigs' brains too).

Albóndigas – pork or beef meatballs, often served in a juicy tomato sauce.

Pinchitos morunos – Moorish meat skewers, marinated in spices and grilled.

Patatas bravas – fried potatoes with spicy tomato or red pepper sauce.

Paella Please

Fry up some rabbit, chicken, duck and snails (optional). Add vegetables, garlic and herbs. Throw in some water, rice and a pinch of yellow saffron, boil it all up and hey presto – paella! This star of Spanish cooking isn't actually a national dish – it comes from the region of Valencia – but you'll find different versions of it all over Spain. Eat straight from the pan for the authentic experience.

With tapas, you can pick and mix!

21

Olé, Olé!

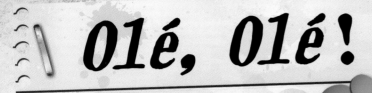

If you're thinking of words that most sum up 'SPAIN', flamenco and bullfighting will be up there! These traditional spectacles began in Andalucía, though they're now part of Spain's whole image. Packed with passion and rippling with rhythm - on the dance floor and in the bullring, drama is the name of the game!

Fiery Music

Flamenco music is fiery stuff, and the most serious kind is *cante jondo*. This means 'deep song', which describes the sound pretty well. A flamenco guitar accompanies the singer; it's lighter than a normal guitar and players tap it like a drum as well as strumming it. In modern flamenco you'll also see the *cajon*, a box-like instrument. Conveniently it doubles as a seat – you just sit on it and slap the front!

A group performs the opera Carmen, set in Spain.

The record for the fastest flamenco feet, set by a woman in Madrid, is 1,274 taps in a minute!

Dynamic Dance

Some say it began with gypsies; others with Muslims or Jews. Whatever its roots, the foot-stamping, skirt-swishing frenzy of flamenco is dizzying both to dance and to watch. Women twirl in big frilly dresses, clicking their fingers or wooden castanets. Men stomp around wearing heeled boots with nails in the soles for extra clunk. If you can't move your feet lightning fast, forget it!

When you watch flamenco, clap to the rhythm of the music!

Dangerous Game

Not everyone wants to watch a bull being baited then killed – but love it or hate it, bullfighting is in Spain's heart. Most cities and towns have a bullring, where brave matadors battle with big-horned beasts in front of excited crowds. While some people say it's a cruel blood sport, others call bullfighting an art. There's certainly plenty of colour, with eye-catching capes and costumes.

The matador's suit is richly embroidered in gold.

23

Hola World!

International fashion icons? Tick. World-famous movie stars? Tick. More than 50 million foreign tourists visiting every year? Tick. Global gossip magazines, car brands, clothing labels, nearly 500 million people speaking its language... Yes, Spain has all these things and more! It's true that times have been hard lately, but this charismatic country still catches the world's eye.

NO WAY!

In the 1960s and 70s, about 150 Westerns were filmed in dusty Almería, in southern Spain. You can still visit the sets at Mini Hollywood.

Spanish Style

You've probably heard of Zara and Mango (you might even be wearing them too!). These popular Spanish labels fly off the shelves in thousands of high-street stores worldwide. You're more likely to see shoes by Manolo Blahnik or clothes by Estrella Archs on catwalks or on the rich and famous. Follow other Spanish designers at fashion weeks in Madrid and Barcelona – they're don't-miss dates in the world style calendar.

A model walks the runway at an Estrella Archs fashion show in Paris.

Screen Sensations

There are some big Spanish names in Hollywood. Think actors like Penélope Cruz, Antonio Banderas and Javier Bardem – not to mention directors such as Pedro Almodóvar and Guillermo del Toro. Films made in Spain attract huge audiences too. In 2012 they had their best year ever, with 163 movies raking in more than 100 million Euros from Spanish screens alone.

Penélope Cruz has a star on the Hollywood Walk of Fame!

Valuable Visitors

People swim and sunbathe on the beach at Lloret de Mar, one of the most popular holiday resorts in Spain.

We know people like to go on holiday to Spain – in fact they prefer it to almost anywhere else! Spain comes third after France and the USA for tourist numbers, and in 2012, 58 million visitors spent nearly 56,000 million Euros between them! The Brits are particularly keen on Spain, making up about a quarter of all visitors. Hot on their heels are Germans and the French.

Eye-Popping Arts

Some places just seem to churn out talent, and Spain is one of them! So many great artists have lived here that you might wonder what's in the water. Luckily there are plenty of spots to admire their work, with world-leading galleries such as the Prado in Madrid. Of course, Spain also has six Nobel Prizes for Literature; and its architecture, well, it's hard to know where to start...

Punchy Painters

He grew a mad moustache, painted melting clocks, made a lobster telephone and designed the Chupa Chups lolly logo. Salvador Dalí was one of Spain's wackier artists. He and his pals Joan Miró (who painted dreams he had when he was starving) and Pablo Picasso (whose portraits look both forwards and sideways) really shook up the art world in the 1900s. Now we'll never forget them!

 Maybe Dalí sat on his Lips Sofa to dial his Lobster Telephone!

Magical Museums

What better way to house Spain's art than in some weird and wonderful buildings. The Dalí Museum in Figueres is a pink and gold castle, with giant eggs teetering on the roof. Bilbao's fish-scale-inspired Guggenheim Museum is an even more eye-catching structure. It contains the latest masterpieces from a load of contemporary artists, and a giant flower-covered puppy guards the outside!

The titanium-clad Guggenheim Museum cost US$89 million to build!

Old but Awesome

Just a few things that might impress you about Spain's older buildings:

In Cuenca there are houses that literally hang off cliffs.

Ronda's Puente Nuevo (a 120-metre-tall bridge) took 43 years to build, with 50 workers reputedly falling to their death.

The Alcázar in Segovia inspired Walt Disney's famous castle.

Fiesta Forever!

Put on your party shoes and dance your way around Spain - you could live one long fiesta here! Festivals (called fiestas) happen in every corner of the country at different times of year. There's something for everyone, from giant food fights to dazzling parades...

You can't be too dressed-up for the Santa Cruz Carnival!

February

At Carnival time people really go crazy – especially in Santa Cruz, Tenerife. Costumes are incredible – the Carnival Queen's can be 6m high and weigh up to 200kg!

Hooded *nazarenos* lead a Semana Santa parade.

March

Semana Santa, the week before Easter, is a flurry of holy parades. Watch floats topped with religious figures travel through the streets, with bands and people in pointy hoods marching too.

March

You spend months crafting a spectacular papier maché figure – then it literally goes up in flames! That's what happens at Las Fallas in Valencia, where burning giant puppets is all part of the show.

April

Seville lights up day and night for its spring fair, or Feria de Sevilla. It's a riot of traditional music, dance and bullfighting. Listen for the click of castanets and shouts of *olé*!

castanets

July

Pamplona is a fairly quiet place – until 6th July. Then rockets fire, champagne corks fly and young men run through the streets, chased by charging bulls! It's San Fermín week.

At San Fermín, there's never a good time to run out of puff!

⟱⟱⟱⟱

NO WAY!

During the Feria de Octubre in Cádiar, Granada, wine flows from the town's fountains instead of water!

August

Food fights don't get messier than Buñol's La Tomatina. People come from far and wide to hurl truckloads of ripe tomatoes at each other! When the missiles run out, they just clear up.

More Information

Websites

http://www.lonelyplanet.com/spain
All you need to prepare for a trip to Spain.

http://www.euroclubschools.co.uk/page15.htm
A long stream of facts, pictures and clips about Spain.

http://www.soccer-spain.com/index.php
Learn about Spanish football, its history, players and what's happening now in the game.

http://www.red2000.com
All about Spain, with lots of info on the different regions.

http://www.bbc.co.uk/news/world-europe-17941641
A country profile by the BBC.

Apps

Spain Travel Guide by Triposo
A complete guide to Spain that works on or offline, this Android app is fully interactive.

Learn Spanish – MindSnacks by MindSnacks
Learn to speak and read Spanish with a set of great games.

Real Football Player Spain by GEM Studios
Dress yourself in the colours of your favourite Spanish team!

Clips

http://video.nationalgeographic.co.uk/video/kids/history-kids/spain-kids/
Take a trip back in time through Spain.

http://www.bbc.co.uk/learningzone/clips/madrid-the-buildings-food-and-flamenco/4113.html
Explore the sights, sounds and tastes of Madrid.

http://www.youtube.com/watch?v=d45uhH2I3xY
A lesson in Basque pelota!

http://www.spain-holiday.com/Spain
A travel company's videos to tempt you to Spain!

Movies

El Alma de la Roja This is a fascinating documentary about the Spanish football team.

El Baño de Papa (The Pope's Toilet) A hilarious film about the preparations of a small South American village for a visit from the Pope.

Rick Stein's Spain This series sees chef Rick Stein travel the length and breadth of Spain in search of the tastiest dishes from each region.

Books

Countries Around the World: Spain by Charlotte Guillain
(Raintree, 2013)

Discover Countries: Spain by Simon Rice
(Wayland, 2010)

Easy Languages: Easy Spanish by Ben Denne and Nicole Irving
(Usborne, 2012)

Sandi Toksvig's Guide to Spain by Sandi Toksvig (Red Fox, 2009)

Toro! Toro! by Michael Morpurgo
(HarperCollins Children's Books, 2007)

Next time you eat a potato, tomato or pineapple, say thanks to Christopher Columbus and his followers for introducing it to Europe!

Glossary

agritourism – Tourism based around farming activities.

Carnival – The festival that's celebrated just before Lent in the Christian calendar.

casas rurales – Meaning 'rural houses'; places where tourists can stay in the Spanish countryside.

castanets – A small percussion instrument made from two pieces of wood, clicked together in one hand.

chorizo – A spicy Spanish pork sausage.

Conquistadors – The Spanish explorers and soldiers who conquered large parts of the Americas in the 1500s.

empire – A group of nations under the power of a single ruler or sovereign country.

export – Something that is shipped and sold abroad.

fiesta – The Spanish word for festival.

fortress – A large building or group of buildings used as a military stronghold.

lava – Molten rock that flows from a volcano and hardens when it cools.

matador – A bullfighter.

monarchy – A country that's ruled by a king, queen or other royal.

paseo – A leisurely stroll, usually taken in the early evening.

rural – Relating to the countryside, rather than towns.

sierra – The Spanish word for a mountain range.

siesta – A rest or nap after lunch.

slum – An overcrowded urban area with poor standards of living.

vineyard – A plantation of grape vines, usually for winemaking.

Index

Unpacked

Australia

Australia: Unpacked
Exploration and Discovery
City Sights
Not All Desert
Aussie Animals
Long Distance Travellers
Go, Aussie, Go!
Mine Time
On the Coast
Native Australians
Aussie Tucker
Everyday Life
Coming to Australia

978 0 7502 7726 6

Brazil

Brazil: Unpacked
A World of Faces
Let's Go to Rio!
Viva Futebol!
Jungle Giant
Nature's Treasure Trove
Highways and Skyways
Bright Lights, Big Cities
Life, Brazilian Style
Looking Good
Arts for All
Adventurous Tastes
Prepare to Party!

978 0 7502 7997 0

France

France: Unpacked
The City of Light
Ruling France
Fruit of the Earth
Home and Away
Power and Progress
Grand Designs
Bon Appetit
The Arts
En Vacance
Made in France
Allez Sport
Life in France

978 0 7502 7728 0

India

India: Unpacked
From 0 to a Billion
Touring India
Everyone's Game
Wild Wonders
Rocks, Rivers, Rains
Life on the Land
High-tech, Low-tech!
Staggering Cities
Everyday India
Spice is Nice
Bollywood Beats
Bright Arts

978 0 7502 7725 9

Italy

Italy: Unpacked
The Romans
Rome: the Eternal City
Way to Go
Food Glorious Food
La Bella Figura
Mountains and Volcanoes
The Italian Arts
Calcio!
North and South
Everyday Life
Super Cities
Italian Inventions

978 0 7502 7727 3

Portugal
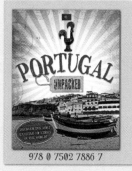
Portugal: Unpacked
Small Country, Big Story
Let's Play!
Holiday Hotspot
Sun, Sand and Serras
Island Magic
Charismatic Cities
Made in Portugal!
Country Corkers
Wild Times
Make Yourself at Home
Surf 'n Turf
Creative Culture

978 0 7502 7886 7

South Africa

South Africa: Unpacked
Three Capitals
The Land
Becoming South Africa
SA Sport
Farming
Rainbow Nation
Fabulous Food
Rich and Poor
Wild Life
Mineral Wealth
On the Coast
Holidays and Festivals

978 0 7502 7729 7

Spain

Spain: Unpacked
A World of Their Own
Fiesta Forever
On the Ball
Highlands and Islands
Sleepless Cities
Escape to the Country
Wild Spain
Spanish Life
All You Can Eat
Hola World!
Olé, Olé!
Eye-Popping Arts

978 0 7502 7730 3

WAYLAND
www.waylandbooks.co.uk